TREATS

just great recipes

D055525

GENERAL INFORMATION

The level of difficulty of the recipes in this book
is expressed as a number from 1 (simple) to 3 (difficult).

TREATS
just great recipes
salads

MⷜRAE BOOKS

SERVES 4

PREPARATION 10 min

DIFFICULTY level 1

Arugula Salad
with pear, brie, and walnuts

Beat the oil, vinegar, and salt with a fork in a small bowl to make a smooth dressing. • Arrange the arugula in a large salad bowl. • Arrange the Brie on the arugula. Top with the slices of pear. • Drizzle with the dressing. Sprinkle with walnuts and serve at once.

$1/4$ cup (60 ml) extra-virgin olive oil
2 tablespoons balsamic vinegar
Salt
5 oz (150 g) arugula (rocket) leaves
8 oz (200 g) Brie, sliced
3 large ripe pears, cored and sliced
16–20 walnuts, coarsely chopped

SERVES 4

PREPARATION 10 min

DIFFICULTY level 1

Mixed Salad

with pear, pecorino, and walnuts

Beat the mustard, vinegar, oil, and salt with a fork in a small bowl to make a smooth dressing. • Place the mixed salad greens and celery in a large salad bowl. • Top with the pears and cover with the Pecorino and walnuts, • Drizzle with the dressing. Toss gently and serve at once.

1 tablespoon French mustard

1 tablespoon white wine vinegar

$\frac{1}{4}$ cup (60 ml) extra-virgin olive oil

Salt

8 oz (250 g) mixed salad greens

2 celery sticks, sliced

2 large ripe pears, peeled, cored, and thinly sliced

4 oz (125 g) aged Pecorino (or Parmesan), cheese cut into flakes

12–16 walnuts, coarsely chopped

SERVES 4–6

PREPARATION 30 min + 45 min to rest

COOKING 50–60 min

DIFFICULTY level 2

Chicken Salad
with pineapple and ham

Fill a large casserole with cold water and bring to a boil. Add the chicken, cloves, sage, bay leaf, rosemary, chopped celery, onion, potato, and carrot. Simmer until the chicken is tender, 45–55 minutes. • Remove the chicken from the casserole and let cool. Reserve the cooking water and vegetables. • Remove and discard the skin. Remove the meat from the bones and place in a large salad bowl. Add the lettuce, shredded celery leaves, ham, apple, and pineapple. Season with salt and pepper. • Drizzle with the lemon juice, toss gently, and let rest for 30 minutes. • Discard the cloves, sage, rosemary, and bay leaf from the reserved stock. • Place 1 cup (250 ml) of the stock and the vegetables in a food processor. Blend until smooth. Add the egg, egg yolks, mustard, and a pinch of salt. Blend until smooth. • Return to the pan and stir constantly over low heat until the sauce thickens, 5–10 minutes. Remove from the heat and stir in the oil. • Drizzle the salad with the dressing. Serve at once.

1 (3 lb/1.5 kg) chicken
2 cloves
3 sage leaves
1 bay leaf
1 sprig of rosemary
4 stalks celery, chopped
1 small onion, chopped
1 potato, peeled and chopped
1 large carrot, peeled and chopped
1 head of lettuce, shredded
2 oz (60 g) celery leaves, shredded
5 oz (150 g) ham, cut into small cubes
1 green apple, cored and cubed
1 small pineapple, peeled, cored, and cut into small cubes
Salt and freshly ground black pepper
Juice of 2 lemons
1 large egg
2 large egg yolks
1 teaspoon wholegrain mustard
1/4 cup (60 ml) extra-virgin olive oil

Citrus Salad
with avocado and yogurt

Arrange the lettuce in a large salad bowl. • Peel the orange and the grapefruit using a sharp knife, removing all the bitter white pith. Break the fruit into segments and add to the bowl with the lettuce. • Cut the avocado in half and remove the pit. Peel and slice into segments. • Drizzle the sliced avocado with the lemon juice to prevent it from turning brown. Add to the salad bowl and toss well. • Beat the yogurt and ricotta in a medium bowl with a fork. Add the chives and Worcestershire sauce and season with salt and pepper. Transfer to a small serving bowl. • Serve the salad with the dressing passed separately.

1 head lettuce, leaves separated and torn
1 large ripe orange
1 large ripe grapefruit
1 large ripe avocado
Juice of 1 lemon
1/2 cup (125 g) plain yogurt
5 oz (150 g) fresh ricotta cheese, drained
2 tablespoons finely chopped chives
1 teaspoon Worcestershire sauce
Salt and freshly ground black pepper

SERVES 4

PREPARATION 15 min

DIFFICULTY level 1

Crab Salad
with pomegranate and orange

Peel the oranges using a sharp knife, removing all the bitter white pith and collecting the juice in a small bowl. Break the fruit into segments and place in a large salad bowl. • Add the arugula, olives, crabmeat, and pomegranate seeds. • Add the lemon juice to the bowl with the orange juice. Stir in the oil and season with salt and pepper. Beat well with a fork. • Drizzle the dressing over the salad. Toss gently before serving.

2 large ripe oranges
4 oz (125 g) arugula (rocket) leaves
1/2 cup (50 g) black olives
4 oz (125 g) cooked (or canned) crabmeat, crumbled
Seeds from 1 large pomegranate
Juice of 1/2 lemon
1/4 cup (60 ml) extra-virgin olive oil
Salt and freshly ground black pepper

SERVES 4–6

PREPARATION 15 min

COOKING 35–40 min

DIFFICULTY level 1

Spelt Salad

with tomatoes, corn, and capers

Cook the spelt in a large pot of salted boiling water until tender, 35–40 minutes. Drain well and cool under cold running water. Drain again and transfer to a clean kitchen cloth. Dry well and place in a large salad bowl. • Add the tomatoes, corn, capers, scallions, parsley, basil, and mint. Toss well. • Beat the oil and lemon juice in a small bowl. Season with salt and pepper. • Drizzle the dressing over the salad. Toss well before serving.

1 lb (500 g) spelt (or pearl barley)
24 cherry tomatoes, cut in half
4 oz (125 g) canned corn (sweetcorn)
2 tablespoons capers preserved in brine
2 scallions (green onions), sliced
1 tablespoon finely chopped parsley
1 tablespoon finely chopped basil
$1/2$ tablespoon finely chopped mint
$1/3$ cup (90 ml) extra-virgin olive oil
Juice of 1 lemon
Salt and freshly ground black pepper

Spelt Salad
with mozzarella and corn

Cook the spelt in a large pot of salted boiling water until tender, 35–40 minutes. Drain well and cool under cold running water. Drain again and transfer to a clean kitchen cloth. Dry well and place in a large salad bowl. • While the spelt is cooking, preheat the broiler (grill) to high. Grill the bell pepper, turning often, until it is charred all over, 15–20 minutes. Wrap the blackened bell pepper in aluminum foil and let rest for 10 minutes. Unwrap and remove the skin and seeds. Rinse under cold water, dry well, and slice thinly. • Add the bell pepper, mozzarella, corn, parsley, basil, marjoram, and garlic to the salad bowl with the spelt. Toss well. • Beat the oil and lemon juice in a small bowl with a fork. Season with salt and pepper. • Drizzle the dressing over the salad. • Toss well before serving.

1 lb (500 g) spelt (or pearl barley)
1 large red bell pepper (capsicum)
8 oz (250 g) fresh mozzarella cheese, drained and cut into small cubes
4 oz (125 g) canned corn (sweetcorn)
1 tablespoon finely chopped parsley
1 tablespoon finely chopped basil
1/2 tablespoon finely chopped marjoram
1 clove garlic, finely chopped
1/3 cup (90 ml) extra-virgin olive oil
Juice of 1 lemon
Salt and freshly ground black pepper

Tuna Salad
with spelt

Cook the spelt in a large pot of salted boiling water until tender, 35–40 minutes. Drain well and cool under cold running water. Drain again and transfer to a clean kitchen cloth. Dry well and place in a large salad bowl. • Add the tomatoes, onion, and tuna. Season with salt and pepper and toss well. • Drizzle with the oil, toss again, and serve.

1 lb (500 g) spelt (or pearl barley)
24 cherry tomatoes, cut in half
1 sweet red onion, finely chopped
8 oz (250 g) canned tuna, drained
1/4 cup (60 ml) extra-virgin olive oil
Salt and freshly ground black pepper

Bean Salad
with onion and bell pepper

Place the beans in a large bowl. • Add the bell pepper, onion, garlic, and parsley and toss well. • Beat the oil and lemon juice in a small bowl with a fork. Season with salt and pepper. • Drizzle the dressing over the salad. Toss well, cover, and let rest for 30 minutes. • Arrange the salad greens in a large salad bowl. • Spoon the bean salad over the top. Garnish with the sprigs of parsley and serve.

1 (14-oz/400-g) can cranberry
    or borlotti beans, drained
1 (14-oz/400-g) can cannellini
    or white kidney beans, drained
1 large red bell pepper (capsicum),
    seeded and finely sliced
1 sweet red onion, sliced finely
1 clove garlic, finely chopped
4 tablespoons finely chopped parsley
    + extra sprigs, to garnish
1/4 cup (60 ml) extra-virgin olive oil
Juice of 1 lemon
Salt and freshly ground black pepper
5 oz (150 g) lollo rosso (or other)
    salad greens

14

Potato Salad
with walnuts and lemon cream

Cook the potatoes in a pan of salted boiling water until tender, 20–30 minutes. Drain well and let cool. • Slip the skins off the potatoes and cut into bite-size cubes. • Place the lettuce and radicchio in a large salad bowl. Top with the potatoes, apple, and walnuts. Season with salt and pepper. Toss gently. • Beat the cream, lemon juice, and vinegar in a medium bowl until thickened. Season with salt and pepper. • Spoon the dressing over the salad and serve.

1 lb (500 g) new potatoes
1 medium head lettuce
  (or other salad greens), torn
1 small head red radicchio,
  coarsely chopped
1 large apple, peeled, cored and diced
25–30 walnuts, coarsely chopped
Salt and freshly ground white pepper
1 cup (250 ml) heavy (double) cream
2 tablespoons fresh lemon juice
$\frac{1}{2}$ tablespoon white wine vinegar

Spinach Salad
with oranges and avocado

Peel the oranges using a sharp knife, removing all the bitter white pith. Break the fruit into segments. • Place the spinach leaves in a large salad bowl. Top with the oranges and avocados. • Beat the lemon juice and oil in a small bowl with a fork. • Add the scallions and orange zest and season with salt and pepper. Beat well. • Drizzle the dressing over the salad and toss carefully. • Serve at once.

2 large ripe oranges
8 oz (250 g) baby spinach leaves
2 large ripe avocados, peeled, pitted, and sliced
Juice of 1 lemon
1/3 cup (90 ml) extra-virgin olive oil
2 scallions (green onions), sliced
Zest of 1 orange, cut in tiny pieces
Salt and freshly ground black pepper

SERVES 4

PREPARATION 15 min

DIFFICULTY level 1

Spinach Salad
with strawberries and almonds

Toast the almonds in a large frying pan over medium heat until golden brown, about 5 minutes. Remove from the heat and let cool. • Place the spinach, strawberries, fennel, and almonds in a large salad bowl. Toss gently. • Beat the lemon juice, orange juice, oil, vinegar, and mustard in a small bowl with a fork. Season with salt and pepper. • Drizzle the dressing over the salad and toss gently. • Serve at once.

$\frac{2}{3}$ cup (100 g) blanched almonds
12 oz (350 g) baby spinach leaves
14 oz (400 g) strawberries, sliced
1 fennel bulb, thinly sliced
Juice of $\frac{1}{2}$ lemon
Juice of 1 orange
$\frac{1}{4}$ cup (60 ml) extra-virgin olive oil
2 tablespoons balsamic vinegar
1 teaspoon French mustard
Salt and freshly ground black pepper

SERVES 4

PREPARATION 15 min

COOKING 10 min

DIFFICULTY level 1

Mixed Salad
with apple, pancetta, and sesame

Sauté the pancetta in a small frying pan over medium heat until lightly browned and crisp, about 5 minutes. Remove from the heat and let cool. • Toast the sesame seeds and cumin seeds in a small frying pan over medium heat until pale golden brown and fragrant, about 3 minutes. Remove from the heat and let cool. • Beat the oil and vinegar in a small bowl with a fork. Season with salt and pepper. • Arrange the lettuce and curly endive in a large salad bowl. Top with the apple, pancetta, and toasted seeds. Toss gently. • Drizzle with the dressing and sprinkle with Parmesan, • Serve at once.

3 oz (90 g) pancetta (or bacon), cut in small dice
1/4 cup (30 g) sesame seeds
1/2 teaspoon cumin seeds
1/4 cup (60 ml) extra-virgin olive oil
2 tablespoons balsamic vinegar
Salt and freshly ground black pepper
8 oz (250 g) lettuce leaves, coarsely chopped
8 oz (250 g) curly endive, coarsely chopped
1 Granny Smith apple, cored and sliced into thin wedges
3 oz (90 g) Parmesan, cut into flakes

SERVES 4–6

PREPARATION 20 min

COOKING 15–20 min

DIFFICULTY level 1

Chicken Salad
with citrus fruit and arugula

If using chicken breasts, place them in a medium saucepan with the carrot, onion, and celery and bring to a boil over medium heat. Season with salt and simmer until the chicken is tender and cooked through, 15–20 minutes. • Remove from the heat and let cool. The cooking liquid will make a good chicken stock. Refrigerate or freeze for later use. • Chop the chicken breasts into bite-size pieces. • Arrange the arugula in a salad bowl. • Peel the orange and the grapefruit using a sharp knife, removing all the bitter white pith and collecting the juice that will drip as you work in a bowl. • Break the fruit into segments and place on top of the arugula. Top with the chicken. • Beat the reserved orange and grapefruit juices with the oil and season with salt and pepper • Garnish the salad with the onion, if liked, and drizzle with the dressing. • Toss gently and serve.

2 boneless skinless chicken breasts, about 1½ lb (750 g) or the same amount of leftover roast or grilled chicken
1 small carrot, chopped
1 small onion, chopped
1 celery stick, chopped
4 cups (1 liter) water
Salt
4 oz (125 g) arugula (rocket)
1 large orange
1 large grapefruit
¼ cup (60 ml) extra-virgin olive oil
Freshly ground black pepper
1 small onion, finely sliced, to garnish (optional)

SERVES 4

PREPARATION 45 min

COOKING 3–5 min

DIFFICULTY level 1

Crudités
with saffron dip

Remove and discard the tops and roots from the scallions. Cut each scallion from the middle, sliding the knife toward the greener end. Repeat this cut several times on each onion and then place in a bowl of iced water. Let rest until the sliced ends curl, about 20 minutes. Drain well. • Cook the cauliflower in a large pot of salted boiling water until just tender, about 3–5 minutes. Drain well and let cool. • Slice the celery, zucchini, and radishes, if using, lengthwise to make thin batons. Slice the onions into rings. Slice the radicchio into thin wedges. • Arrange the prepared vegetables around the edge of a large serving dish. • Combine the saffron, lemon juice, and horseradish in a small bowl. Season with salt and pepper. Add the oil and ricotta and beat until all the ingredients are well mixed. Stir in the pistachios. • Place the bowl of dip in the center of the serving dish with the vegetables and serve.

4 scallions (green onions)
1 small cauliflower, cut into florets
4–6 tender celery sticks, taken from the heart
8 baby zucchini (courgettes), if possible, with flowers still attached
4 oz (125 g) radishes (optional)
2 small red onions
2 small heads red radicchio
Pinch of saffron strands
2 tablespoons fresh lemon juice
1 tablespoon horseradish
Salt and freshly ground black pepper
$\frac{1}{3}$ cup (90 ml) extra-virgin olive oil
8 oz (250 g) ricotta cheese, drained
4 tablespoons blanched pistachios, chopped

SERVES 2–4

PREPARATION 15 min

DIFFICULTY level 1

Tuna Salad
with beans

Place the tuna in a medium bowl and break it up with a fork. • Add the beans, onion, parsley, and cilantro and toss well. • Arrange the lettuce leaves so that they line the base and sides of a medium salad bowl. Spoon the bean and tuna mixture into the lettuce leaves. • Place the oil, mustard, lemon juice, salt, and pepper in a small bowl and beat well with a fork. • Drizzle over the salad and serve at once.

8 oz (250 g) tuna, canned
1 (14-oz/400-g) can cannellini or white kidney beans, drained
1 sweet red onion, sliced
2 tablespoons finely chopped parsley
1 tablespoon finely chopped cilantro (coriander)
1 small head lettuce or other salad greens
$1/4$ cup (60 ml) extra-virgin olive oil
2 teaspoons French mustard
Juice of 1 lemon
Salt and freshly ground black pepper

Bulgur Salad
with snow peas and herbs

Place the bulgur and 2–3 pinches of salt in a medium bowl and pour the boiling water in over the top. Stir gently, then cover with a clean cloth. Let stand until the bulgur is tender, 20–25 minutes. • While the bulgur is soaking, boil the snow peas in a small saucepan of lightly salted water until tender, 5–7 minutes. Drain and let cool. • Squeeze any excess water out of the bulgur and place in a salad bowl. • Add the snow peas, scallions, cucumber, tomatoes, onion, parsley, and mint. Toss gently. • Beat the oil, lemon juice, salt, and pepper in a small bowl. Drizzle over the salad and toss gently. • Chill the salad in the refrigerator for 1 hour before serving.

1 cup (150 g) medium-grain bulgur
Salt
2½ cups (625 ml) boiling water
4 oz (125 g) snow peas (mangetout) finely sliced
2 scallions (green onions, finely sliced
1 cucumber, peeled and cut in tiny dice
2 ripe tomatoes, cut in small dice
1 small sweet red onion, finely chopped
4–6 tablespoons finely chopped parsley
1 tablespoon finely chopped mint
¼ cup (60 ml) extra-virgin olive oil
Juice of 1 lemon
Freshly ground black pepper

SERVES 4

PREPARATION 20 min

COOKING 5 min

DIFFICULTY level 1

Pineapple Salad
with peanuts and bean sprouts

Place the pineapple, bean sprouts, peanuts, carrots, and scallions in a large salad bowl. Toss gently. • Place the peanut butter, oil, soy sauce, vinegar, and chile in a small saucepan over low heat. Stir gently until well mixed, adding enough water to obtain a smooth, creamy dressing. • Spoon the dressing over the salad, or serve separately in a small bowl so that guests can serve themselves.

8 oz (250 g) fresh or canned pineapple, cut in bite-size pieces
8 oz (250 g) bean sprouts
1 cup (100 g) toasted peanuts
2 large carrots, grated
1 small cucumber, peeled and diced
2 scallions (green onions), finely sliced
6 tablespoons smooth peanut butter
2 tablespoons vegetable oil
2 teaspoons light soy sauce
1 teaspoon white vinegar
1 teaspoon ground chile (or 1 fresh red chile pepper, finely sliced)
About $\frac{1}{2}$ cup (125 ml) cold water

SERVES 4
PREPARATION 30 min
COOKING 45 min
DIFFICULTY level 2

Baked Rice Salad
with peas, green beans, and corn

Preheat the oven to 350°F (180°C/gas 4). • Stud the onion with the cloves. • Heat 2 tablespoons of the oil in a large casserole over medium heat. Add the onion and sauté for 3–4 minutes. • Add the rice and mix well. Add the bay leaf and stock. • Cover and bake until the rice has absorbed all the stock and is al dente, about 20 minutes. • Remove from the oven and let cool. • Meanwhile, cook the green beans in a medium pot of salted boiling water until just tender, 5–7 minutes. Drain well and let cool. • Cook the peas in a small pot of salted boiling water until just tender, 3–5 minutes. Drain well and let cool. • Preheat the broiler (grill) to high. Grill the bell pepper, turning often, until charred all over, 15–20 minutes. Wrap the blackened bell pepper in aluminum foil and let rest for 10 minutes. Unwrap and remove the skin and seeds. Rinse under cold water, dry well, and slice thinly. • Put the gherkins, capers, remaining oil, and vinegar into a food processor. Blend until smooth. • Transfer the rice to a large salad bowl. Remove and discard the onion, cloves, and bay leaf. Add the green beans, peas, corn, pepper, and arugula. • Drizzle with the dressing and toss gently. • Serve lukewarm.

1 small onion
3 cloves
1/3 cup (90 ml) extra-virgin olive oil
1 1/2 cups (300 g) short-grain rice
1 bay leaf
Generous 2 1/3 cups (600 ml) vegetable stock, boiling
5 oz (150 g) fresh or frozen green beans, chopped
5 oz (150 g) fresh or frozen peas
1 large red pepper (capsicum)
6 pickled gherkins, drained and chopped
1 tablespoon salt cured capers, rinsed
3 tablespoons white wine vinegar
Salt
5 oz (150 g) canned corn (sweetcorn)
4 oz (125 g) arugula (rocket), chopped

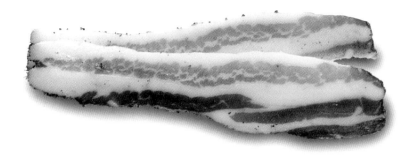

SERVES 4

PREPARATION 20 min

COOKING 10 min

DIFFICULTY level 1

Crisp Salad
with pancetta, avocado, and nuts

Melt the butter in a large frying pan over medium heat. Add the pancetta and sauté until browned and crisp, about 5 minutes. • Transfer the pancetta to a layer of paper towels using a slotted spoon and let cool. • Add the bread to the frying pan and sauté until golden brown and crisp, about 3 minutes. Remove from the heat and let cool. • Place the salad greens in a large salad bowl. Add the pancetta, hazelnuts, and avocado. • Beat the oil, balsamic vinegar, and mustard in a small bowl with a fork. Season with salt and pepper. • Drizzle the dressing over the salad and toss gently. • Sprinkle with the croutons and serve at once.

1 tablespoon butter

8 oz (250 g) pancetta (or bacon), cut in small cubes

8 slices white bread, cut into small cubes

12 oz (350 g) mixed salad greens

1 cup (100 g) coarsely chopped hazelnuts

1 large ripe avocado, peeled, pitted, and cut in small cubes

1/4 cup (60 ml) extra-virgin olive oil

1 tablespoon balsamic vinegar

1 tablespoon French mustard

Salt and freshly round black pepper

Caribbean Salad

with chicken and ginger

If using chicken breasts, place them in a medium saucepan with the carrot, onion, and celery and bring to a boil over medium heat. Season with salt and simmer until the chicken is tender and cooked through, 15–20 minutes. • Remove from the heat and let cool. The cooking liquid will make a good chicken stock. Refrigerate or freeze for later use. • Chop the chicken breasts into bite-size pieces. • Boil the eggs for 8 minutes from the moment the water reaches a boil. Drain and cool under cold running water. Shell and cut into segments. • Toast the almonds in a frying pan over medium heat until golden brown, 3–4 minutes. Let cool. • Place the chicken and almonds in a large salad bowl. Add the endive, arugula, pineapple, ham, and eggs. • Dressing: Cut the avocado in half and remove the pit. Scoop out the flesh and chop in a food processor with the lemon juice, garlic, scallion, salt, and pepper until smooth. • Gradually add the oil, blending continuously, to make a smooth creamy dressing. Drizzle the dressing over the salad and toss well. • Serve at once.

2 boneless skinless chicken breasts,
about 1½ lb (750 g),
or the same amount of leftover
roast or grilled chicken
1 small carrot, peeled and chopped
1 small onion, chopped
1 celery stick, chopped
4 large eggs
2 tablespoons blanched almonds
2 heads endive, sliced
8 oz (250 g) arugula (rocket), chopped
4 oz (125 g) fresh pineapple, peeled,
cored, and chopped
5 oz (150 g) ham,
cut into ribbons
1 small ripe avocado
Juice of 1 lemon
1 clove garlic, chopped
1 scallion (green onion), chopped
Salt and freshly ground black pepper
⅓ cup (90 ml) extra-virgin olive oil

SERVES 4
PREPARATION 15 min
COOKING 15 min
DIFFICULTY level 1

Fusilli Salad
with cherry tomatoes and ricotta

Cook the pasta in a large pot of salted boiling water until al dente.
• Beat together the ricotta, oil, garlic, and basil in a large salad bowl
to make a smooth dressing. Season with salt and pepper. Mix well.
• Drain the pasta and cool under cold running water. Drain again
and dry on a clean kitchen cloth. • Add the pasta and tomatoes to
the bowl with the dressing. Toss well. • Garnish with basil and serve.

12 oz (350 g) ricotta cheese, drained
1/3 cup (90 ml) extra-virgin olive oil
1 clove garlic, finely chopped
20 basil leaves, torn
    + extra, to garnish
Salt and freshly ground black pepper
1 lb (500 g) fusilli (or other short
    pasta shape)
20 cherry tomatoes, halved

SERVES 4

PREPARATION 10 min + 30 min to rest

COOKING 15 min

DIFFICULTY level 1

Penne Salad
with tomatoes and mozzarella

Place the tomatoes, mozzarella, garlic, oil, and basil in a large salad bowl. Mix well and let rest for 30 minutes. • Cook the pasta in a large pot of salted boiling water until al dente. • Drain well and cool under cold running water. Drain again and dry on a clean kitchen cloth. • Add the pasta to the bowl with the dressing. Remove and discard the garlic. Toss well. • Garnish with basil and serve.

1½ lb (750 g) cherry tomatoes, halved

14 oz (400 g) fresh mozzarella balls, drained

1 clove garlic, lightly crushed but whole

⅓ cup (90 ml) extra-virgin olive oil

Leaves from 4 sprigs of basil, torn, + extra, to garnish

1 lb (500 g) penne (or other short pasta shape)

Pasta Salad

with feta, garlic, and black olives

Place the tomatoes, onion, garlic, feta, oil, basil, mint, and lemon zest in a large salad bowl. Toss well and season with salt and pepper. Let rest for 30 minutes. • Cook the pasta in a large pot of salted boiling water until al dente. • Drain well and cool under cold running water. Drain again and dry on a clean kitchen cloth. • Add the pasta to the bowl with the dressing. Add the olives and toss well. • Garnish with basil and serve.

1½ lb (750 g) cherry tomatoes, quartered

1 small red onion, finely sliced

1 clove garlic, finely chopped

8 oz (250 g) feta cheese, cut into small cubes

⅓ cup (90 ml) extra-virgin olive oil

1 tablespoon finely chopped basil, + extra sprigs, to garnish

1 tablespoon finely chopped mint

Grated zest of 1 lemon

Salt and freshly ground black pepper

1 lb (500 g) penne or other short pasta shape

1 cup (100 g) black olives, pitted

SERVES 4

PREPARATION 10 min

COOKING 25 min

DIFFICULTY level 1

Fusilli Salad
with peas and hazelnuts

Cook the pasta in a large pot of salted boiling water until al dente. • Drain well and cool under cold running water. Drain again and dry on a clean kitchen cloth. Transfer to a large salad bowl. • Cook the peas in a large pot of salted boiling until tender, about 5 minutes. Drain well and cool under cold running water. Drain well and add to the bowl with the pasta. • Beat the oil and mustard in a small bowl with a fork. • Drizzle over the salad and season with salt and pepper. Toss well. • Add the hazelnuts and Pecorino and toss again. • Garnish with parsley and serve.

1 lb (500 g) fusilli pasta
2 cups (300 g) fresh or frozen peas
1/4 cup (60 ml) extra-virgin olive oil
1 tablespoon French mustard
Salt and freshly ground black pepper
1/3 cup (50 g) chopped hazelnuts
5 oz (150 g) aged Pecorino cheese, cut into flakes
1 tablespoon finely chopped parsley, to garnish

Chicken Salad

with avocado and champignons

If using chicken breasts, cook them following the instructions on page 34. • Chop the chicken into bite-size pieces and place in a large salad bowl. • Peel and pit the avocado and cut into small cubes. Drizzle with the lemon juice. • Top the chicken with the scallions, avocado, and mushrooms. • Beat the oil, orange juice, salt, and pepper in a small bowl with a fork. • Drizzle over the salad, toss gently, and serve at once.

2 boneless skinless chicken breasts, about 1½ lb (750 g) or the same amount of leftover roast or grilled chicken

2 scallions (green onions), sliced

1 medium avocado

Juice of 1 lemon

4 oz (125 g) champignons (button mushrooms), cleaned and sliced

2 tablespoons finely chopped basil

⅓ cup (90 ml) extra-virgin olive oil

Juice of 1 orange

Salt and freshly ground black pepper

SERVES 4

PREPARATION 30 min

COOKING 5–7 min

DIFFICULTY level 2

Spicy Fish Salad
with tortillas

Steam the fish over medium heat until cooked through, 5–7 minutes. • Remove from the heat and let cool. Break the fish into flakes, removing any bones. • Cut the avocado in half and remove the pit. Peel the avocado and slice thinly. Drizzle with half the lemon juice to prevent it from browning. • Beat the chile pepper oil and remaining lemon juice in a small bowl with a fork. Season with salt. • Place the endive, tomatoes, pepper, fish, avocado, and tortilla chips in a large salad bowl. • Drizzle with the dressing, toss gently, and serve at once.

1 lb (500 g) cleaned salmon
   or cod fillets
1 large ripe avocado
Juice of 1 lemon
$\frac{1}{4}$ cup (60 ml) spicy chile pepper oil
Salt
1 head endive, sliced
4 ripe tomatoes, cut into wedges
1 large yellow bell pepper (capsicum),
   seeded and sliced
3 oz (90 g) tortilla chips

SERVES 4

PREPARATION 20 min

DIFFICULTY level 1

Cheese Salad
with fresh fruit and herbs

Place both cheeses in a large salad bowl. • Add the lettuce, radicchio, endive, apple, pear, grapes, sultanas, orange, and grapefruit. Toss well. • Beat the oil and vinegar in a small bowl with a fork. Add the mustard, dill, chives, parsley, and tarragon. Season with salt and pepper and beat again. • Drizzle the salad with the dressing and toss gently. • Serve at once.

4 oz (125 g) Emmental or other mild cheese, cut into small cubes
4 oz (125 g) aged Pecorino or Parmesan, cut into flakes
4 oz (125 g) lettuce, chopped
1 small radicchio, shredded
1 head curly endive, chopped
1 apple, peeled, cored, and cut into small cubes
1 pear, peeled, cored, and cut into small cubes
3 oz (90 g) green grapes, halved
2 tablespoons golden raisins (sultanas)
1 orange, peeled and cut in segments
1 pink grapefruit, peeled and cut in segments
1 shallot, finely chopped
$1/4$ cup (60 ml) extra-virgin olive oil
1 tablespoon balsamic vinegar
1 tablespoon wholegrain mustard
2 tablespoons finely chopped dill
2 tablespoons finely chopped chives
2 tablespoons finely chopped parsley
1 tablespoon finely chopped tarragon
Salt and freshly ground white pepper

Tuna Salad

with olives, eggs, and fava beans

Place the eggs in a saucepan and cover with water. Bring to a boil over medium heat. Cook for 8 minutes from the moment the water reaches a boil. Drain and cool under cold running water. Shell the eggs and cut into segments. • Place the tomatoes, peppers, celery, onion, radishes, and cucumber in a large salad bowl. Add the olives, fava beans, and garlic. Toss well. • Add the tuna, eggs, and anchovies. • Beat the oil and vinegar in a small bowl with a fork. Add the basil and season with salt and pepper. Beat again and then drizzle over the salad. • Toss gently before serving.

2 large eggs

3 ripe tomatoes, cut into segments

2 red bell peppers (capsicums), seeded and sliced

1 celery stick, sliced

1 small red onion, sliced

6 radishes, sliced

1 cucumber, peeled and sliced

$^1\!/_2$ cup (50 g) black olives, pitted

$^1\!/_2$ cup (50 g) green olives, pitted

1 lb (500 g) fresh fava (broad) beans, shelled

2 cloves garlic, finely chopped

8 oz (250 g) canned tuna, drained and crumbled

12 anchovy fillets, chopped

$^1\!/_3$ cup (90 ml) extra-virgin olive oil

3 tablespoons white wine vinegar

10 basil leaves, torn

Salt and freshly ground black pepper

Capri Salad

Place the mozzarella in a large salad bowl. • Add the garlic, tomatoes, oil, and balsamic vinegar, if using. Season with salt and pepper. Toss well and then sprinkle with the basil leaves. • Let rest for 15 minutes before serving.

8 oz (250 g) fresh buffalo mozzarella, drained and cut into small cubes
1 clove garlic, finely chopped
1 lb (500 g) cherry tomatoes, halved
$^1\!/_4$ cup (60 ml) extra-virgin olive oil
1 tablespoon balsamic vinegar (optional)
Salt and freshly ground black pepper
15 basil leaves

Salad Niçoise

Preheat the oven to 350°F (180°C/gas 4) • Put the bread on an oiled baking sheet and toast in the oven until crisp and golden brown. Let cool. • Cook the beans in a large pot of salted boiling water until tender, 5–7 minutes. Drain and let cool. • Put the tomatoes, anchovies, bell pepper, beans, capers, olives, scallion, and tuna into a large bowl. • Beat the oil and vinegar in a small bowl with a fork. Add the garlic, tarragon, parsley, salt, and pepper. Beat well. • Drizzle over the salad and toss gently. • Line a large salad bowl with the lettuce leaves. Spoon the salad over the lettuce. Top with the eggs and croutons and serve.

4 slices white bread, cut in small cubes
8 oz (250 g) green beans, cut in short lengths
8 oz (250 g) tomatoes, sliced
2 anchovy fillets preserved in oil, drained and chopped
1 red bell pepper (capsicum), seeded and sliced
1 tablespoon capers preserved in salt, rinsed
½ cup (50 g) black olives, pitted
1 scallion (green onion), sliced
4 oz (125 g) tuna preserved in oil, drained and crumbled
1 tablespoon white wine vinegar
¼ cup (60 ml) extra-virgin olive oil
1 clove garlic, finely chopped
1 tablespoon finely chopped tarragon
1 tablespoon finely chopped parsley
Salt and freshly ground black pepper
8 large lettuce leaves
4 hard-boiled eggs, sliced

Chicken Salad
with pomegranate

If using chicken breasts, place in a medium saucepan with the carrot, onion, and celery and bring to a boil over medium heat. Season with salt and simmer until the chicken is tender and cooked through, 15–20 minutes. • Remove from the heat and let cool. The cooking liquid will make a good chicken stock. Refrigerate or freeze for later use. • Chop the chicken breasts into bite-size pieces. • Place the chicken in a large salad bowl with the mixed salad greens. • Beat the oil and lemon juice in a small bowl with a fork. Add the cilantro, parsley, and chives. Season with salt and toss well • Add the pomegranate to the salad bowl and season with pepper. • Drizzle with the dressing and toss again. • Sprinkle with the Parmesan and serve at once.

2 boneless skinless chicken breasts, about 1 1/2 lb (750 g), or the same amount of leftover roast or grilled chicken
1 small carrot, peeled and chopped
1 small onion, chopped
1 celery stick, chopped
8 oz (250 g) mixed salad greens
1/3 cup (90 ml) extra-virgin olive oil
Juice of 1 lemon
2 tablespoons finely chopped cilantro (coriander)
1 tablespoon finely chopped parsley
1/2 tablespoon finely chopped chives
Salt
Seeds from 1 large pomegranate
Freshly ground black pepper
4 oz (125 g) Parmesan, cut into flakes

Ham Salad
with apple, cheese, and sour cream

Place the apples in a large salad bowl. Drizzle with the lemon juice and toss gently to prevent them from turning brown. • Beat the horseradish and sour cream in a small bowl with a fork. Season with salt and pepper. • Add the prosciutto, Fontina, and spring onions to the bowl with the apples. • Drizzle with the dressing, toss gently and serve at once.

2 large ripe apples, peeled, cored, and cut into small cubes
Juice of ½ lemon
1 tablespoon horseradish
½ cup (125 ml) sour cream
Salt and freshly ground black pepper
4 oz (125 g) prosciutto (Parma ham), cut in thin strips
5 oz (150 g) Fontina or other mild firm cheese, cut into small cubes
2 scallions (green onions), sliced

Artichoke Salad
with parmesan

Clean the artichokes by pulling the tough outer leaves down and snapping them off. Cut off the top third of the leaves and trim the stalk. Cut in half and use a sharp knife to remove any fuzzy choke. • Place artichokes in a medium bowl. Drizzle with three-quarters of the lemon juice. Cover with cold water and let soak for 15 minutes. • Drain the artichokes and slice finely. • Transfer to a large salad bowl. Add the carrot and celery. Drizzle with the remaining lemon juice and toss gently. • Drizzle with the oil and season with salt and pepper. Top with the Parmesan, toss gently, and serve.

4 artichokes
juice of 2 lemons
1 large carrot, cut into julienne strips
1 small head of celery, finely sliced
1/4 cup (60 ml) extra-virgin olive oil
Salt and freshly ground black pepper
4 oz (125 g) Parmesan cut into flakes

SERVES 4

PREPARATION 15 min

DIFFICULTY level 1

Arugula Salad

with parmesan and red apple

Place the arugula in a large salad bowl. Top with the Parmesan. • Cut the apple in half, remove the core, and cut into small dice. Drizzle with the lemon juice and add to the salad. Sprinkle with the walnuts. • Place the oil, vinegar, and mustard in a small bowl. Season with salt and pepper and beat with a fork until well mixed. • Drizzle the dressing over the salad. Toss gently and serve at once.

6 oz (180 g) arugula (rocket)
4 oz (125 g) Parmesan, in flakes
1 large red Delicious apple
Juice of $\frac{1}{2}$ lemon
16 walnuts, coarsely chopped
$\frac{1}{4}$ cup (60 ml) extra-virgin olive oil
2 tablespoons white wine vinegar
1 teaspoon French mustard
Salt and freshly ground black pepper

SERVES 4

PREPARATION 20 min

COOKING 15 min

DIFFICULTY level 1

Vegetable Salad
with black olives

Cook the potatoes in a pot of salted boiling water until tender, about 10 minutes. Let cool. • Clean the artichokes by pulling the tough outer leaves down and snapping them off. Cut off the top third of the leaves and trim the stalk. Cut in half and use a sharp knife to remove any fuzzy choke. • Cook the artichokes, carrots, and peas in a large pot of salted boiling water until tender, 5–7 minutes. • Run under cold running water to cool. Drain well. • Place the potatoes, artichokes, carrots, and peas in a large salad bowl. Top with the cheese and season with salt and pepper. Toss gently. • Place the oil and lemon juice in a small bowl and beat well with a fork. Drizzle the dressing over the salad. • Sprinkle with the parsley, capers, and olives. • Serve at once.

3 large potatoes, peeled and cut in small cubes
3 artichokes
2 large carrots, peeled and cut into small cubes
1 cup (150 g) fresh or frozen peas
4 oz (125 g) Edam or other mild, firm cheese, cut into small cubes
Salt and freshly ground black pepper
6 tablespoons extra-virgin olive oil
Juice of 1 lemon
1 tablespoon finely chopped parsley
1 tablespoon capers in brine, drained
Handful of black olives, pitted

Tomato Salad
with cucumber, onions, and olives

Place the onions in a salad bowl and season with salt. • Add the tomatoes, cucumber, bell pepper, and chile pepper. • Place the oil and lemon juice in a small bowl and beat with a fork until well mixed. Season with salt and pepper. • Drizzle the dressing over the salad and toss well. • Garnish with the olives and serve at once.

2 medium onions, thinly sliced
Salt and freshly ground black pepper
4–6 large salad tomatoes, coarsely chopped
1 cucumber, peeled and cubed
1 green bell pepper (capsicum), seeded and cut in small pieces
1 fresh red chile pepper, finely sliced
1/3 cup (90 ml) extra-virgin olive oil
2 tablespoons fresh lemon juice
Black olives, to garnish

ERVES 4

PREPARATION ... ... to cool

G 25 min

Y level 1

Potato Salad
with garlic and mint

Boil the potatoes in their skins in a large pot of salted boiling water until tender, about 25 minutes. • Drain well, let cool enough to handle, then slip off the skins. • Chop into bite-size pieces and transfer to a large salad bowl. Let cool. • Add the mint and garlic. Toss well. • Place the oil and vinegar in a small bowl and beat well with a fork. Drizzle over the potatoes. Season with salt and pepper and serve.

8 medium potatoes
1 tablespoon finely chopped mint
2 cloves garlic, finely chopped
1/4 cup (60 ml) extra-virgin olive oil
2 tablespoons white wine vinegar
Salt and freshly ground black pepper

Russian Salad

Add 1 tablespoon of vinegar to a saucepan of salted boiling water. Add the potatoes and simmer until tender, about 5 minutes. • Drain and set aside to cool. • Add the peas, green beans, carrots, and remaining vinegar to another saucepan filled with salted boiling water. Simmer until the vegetables are tender, about 5 minutes. • Drain and set aside to cool. • Slice the pickled gherkins into ¼-inch (5-mm) thick wheels. • When the vegetables are cool, place in a large bowl. Mix in the gherkins and capers. Season with salt and pepper, drizzle with the oil and toss gently. • Add three-quarters of the mayonnaise and stir gently until well mixed. • Spoon the salad onto a large serving dish and pipe the remaining mayonnaise around the edges in a decorative manner. Garnish with the peas and lemon, if liked. • Chill in the refrigerator for 15 minutes before serving.

2 tablespoons white wine vinegar
2 large potatoes, peeled and cut in small cubes
6 oz (180 g) fresh or frozen green beans, cut in short lengths
2 large carrots, cut in small cubes
1 cup (150 g) fresh or frozen peas
8 pickled gherkins
1 tablespoon pickled capers, drained
Salt and freshly ground white pepper
4 tablespoons extra-virgin olive oil
1 cup (150 g) mayonnaise
Fresh peas in pod, to garnish (optional)
Slices of lemon, to garnish(optional)

Index

Copyright © 2007 by McRae Books Srl

This English edition first published in 2007

All rights reserved. No part of this book may be reproduced in any form without the prior written permission of the publisher and copyright owner.

Salads

was created and produced by McRae Books Srl

Borgo Santa Croce, 8 – Florence (Italy)

info@mcraebooks.com

Publishers: Anne McRae and Marco Nardi

Project Director: Anne McRae

Design: Sara Mathews

Text: Carla Bardi

Editing: Osla Fraser

Photography: Cristina Canepari, Keeho Casati, Gil Gallo, Walter Mericchi, Sandra Preussinger

Home Economist: Benedetto Rillo

Artbuying: McRae Books

Layouts: Adina Stefania Dragomir

Repro: Fotolito Raf, Florence

ISBN 978-88-89272-89-3

Printed and bound in China